CSU Poetry Series LVII

Buried Treasure

poems by Dan Bellm

Cleveland State University Poetry Center

ALSO BY DAN BELLM

A Story in a Bottle (chapbook, 1991)
Terrain (chapbook, with Molly Fisk and Forrest Hamer, 1998)
One Hand on the Wheel (1999)

Translation:
Angel's Kite / La Estrella de Angel, by Alberto Blanco (1994)

Copyright © 1999 by Dan Bellm
Manufactured in the United States of America

Published by Cleveland State University Poetry Center
1983 East 24th Street
Cleveland, OH 44115-2440

ISBN: 1-880834-46-4 (paper)
      1-880834-47-2 (cloth)

Library of Congress Catalog
Card Number: 99-74284

The Ohio Arts Council helped fund this program with state tax dollars to encourage economic growth, educational excellence and cultural enrichment for all Ohioans.

Buried Treasure

ACKNOWLEDGMENTS

Some of the poems in this book, often in earlier versions, have appeared or are scheduled to appear in the following periodicals:

Americas Review: "Song for two voices."
Caesura: "Aspens."
Manoa: "The last hour of the night."
Negative Capability: "Saints behind glass."
Passages North: "Not there," "Passage."
Poetry: "Silence."
Poetry Flash: "True story."
Poetry Now: "The dead" (as "Hanapepe").
The Santa Clara Review: "A messenger spirit."
Sifrut: "Brand new."
The Threepenny Review: "Buried treasure."
Yalobusha Review: "Siren song."

"Buried treasure" and "A messenger spirit" appeared in earlier form in the chapbook, *A Story in a Bottle* (San Francisco: Norton Coker Press, 1991). "The dead" (as "Hanapepe"), "The last hour of the night," "Silence," "Siren song" and "True story" appeared in the chapbook, *Terrain*, by Dan Bellm, Molly Fisk and Forrest Hamer (Nevada City, CA: Hip Pocket Press, 1998). "Song for two voices" was reprinted in *The Forward*. "Transfigured" appeared in *A Day for a Lay: A Century of Gay Poetry* (New York: Barricade, 1999).

"Aspens" won the 1998 Caesura Prize, judged by Mark Doty. "Saints behind glass" was awarded the Daniel Varoujan Prize in 1993 by the New England Poetry Club, judged by Sue Walker.

My deepest thanks, as ever, to Molly Fisk, Forrest Hamer, the Squaw Valley Community of Writers, and Yoel Kahn.

This collection, in an earlier form, won the 1995 Alice Fay Di Castagnola Award of the Poetry Society of America, judged by Jane Miller.

for Yoel

Blessed are they who remember
that what they now have they once longed for

Jean Valentine
"The River at Wolf"

CONTENTS

SILENCE	3
A MESSENGER SPIRIT	5
LETTING THE BOAT DRIFT	7
SIREN SONG	9
BURIED TREASURE	12
THE LAST HOUR OF THE NIGHT	14
SONG FOR TWO VOICES	16
THE DEAD	18
TRUE STORY	20
TRANSFIGURED	21
ASPENS	25
NOT THERE	33
PASSAGE	34
SAINTS BEHIND GLASS	36
BRAND NEW	46
DELLE AVENUE	55
NOTES TO THE POEMS	73

SILENCE

in memoriam John Cage

Just a few lights on at the camp across the lake —
        no boats — no voices — no birds — no wind —
              and nothing but light reaches us this far
from the deafening stars which aren't even there
            any more — it's a silence we never know
      in the city but there's still the sound of the mountain
                falling and the valley rising up,
        the sound of the heart and breath,
the sound of thought travelling from nowhere
              to the roar inside the ear —
        there is no such thing as silence —
    which at least is what the dead
            composer used to say but what would he say now?
Tonight we are mad at each other and everyone and selfish
        and want to be left alone
      but there is no such thing as alone,
          and though we want to be on vacation
from whatever it is we do when we are not on vacation
      there is no such thing as a vacation —
          the baby wakes up
    at 1 and 2 and 5 a.m.
because his body can't stop moving all night
      because it's growing, because he's learning to walk,
          because he has nothing to get away and rest from
              and there is no such thing as rest —

       this morning when he took six seven eight steps
              across the kitchen and sat down
plop and clapped his hands like wingbeats
    of a bandtailed pigeon taking off over
        treetops his happiness made us both
happy a moment — we had been sitting
        miserably peacefully furious in the silence
     between one wave clapping at the dock and the next —
          there is no such thing as silence —

A MESSENGER SPIRIT

for James Schuyler

Once you start looking there's no end to it — spring day on
      Chimney Rock high above the ocean
facing the wind, a meadow of wildflowers breathing. There are
      violet patches of sea where clouds
pass over the turquoise and green. Pacific ocean, so inviting
      and frightening, like a soul-eye,
like a place of rest. Now I have nothing but his voice in his
      books, endless or not. In the morning
I picked up the paper to read that he died, my father-poet
      and teacher, my old friend I never met,
my old seer. This must be why we learned to fly, the desire
      to walk and run to reach the end
of the land, arrive and then keep going like the loons and
      cormorants gliding over the rocky tops of
tiny islands out there, lines of light on the ocean flashing.
      "Then there is a fifth season, called — but
that's my secret. Yes, my secret, and I'm going to keep it
      that way. Yes, my secret." Dusty ratty pink
checker-bloom; all day I mistook it for some kind of geranium
      until Peterson's field guide scolded
as if any fool in California'd know it's the "very common"
      mallow *sidalcea malvaeflora*. Cat's ear —
a mariposa tulip with cottony hair inside, pale lavender —
      blue-eyed grass, miner's lettuce in
the shrubs' shade, a carpet of blooming ice plant, California
      buttercups, Martin's paintbrush, Douglas's
iris ("top of ovary nipplelike"), red maids — purple, really,

    so delicate and easy to miss with their
brilliant red hearts and why do we want to know their names
    so much? What a dominion of words in our
minds. What a long fall down this brittle scrubbly cliff to
    the waves on the black slate. One night
I remember a red fox appeared at the edge of camp out here
    in the beam of my flashlight: calm,
didn't freeze or startle, just nosed the grass and the knobby
    roots of oaks, padded slowly off through
ferns and down into a canyon. Now I have nothing of you
    but your poems in my hands and your voice in
my ear carrying for hours even in this rough wind. Last night
    you were in my dream like a messenger
spirit: you'd sent me an envelope full of photographs
    so tiny I couldn't see you in them
and once they started blowing out to sea there was no
    end to it, you were here and gone.

LETTING THE BOAT DRIFT

They disappear under the surface
and reappear impossibly far,
their neckrings and the ends of their wings
flash white in the sun, they dive
and surface impossibly near,
curious, watching also for you,
like the idea of happiness, like the idea
that you could be contented in your body
and live in it, in the still water
of a mid-July almost cloudless day,
letting the boat drift —
The loons dive in their cove, alone,
and sometimes re-gather, toward the center of things;
the boat drifts into the inlet
where you fell in love so many years ago
and as you kissed him to seal the pact
ran aground on a very large rock
the earth had hid there by accident, for you,
so that you would laugh, so you would give in,
and kiss him again —
It could have taken all of your life,
and more than that, and longer than that,
to agree to happiness,
just five simple minutes undisturbed by irony or shame,
that you had struck already against some shallow part,
that you had not been watchful enough,
but you agreed to it,
and the loons who are not much concerned with irony

or happiness but only with living and the furtherance
of living call across great distances over the water
in the north-country voices you want to call mournful
or lonely, as if they were ghosts,
because the dead and the living, this time
and all others, the seen and unseen
do stay and rest beside each other
always and at once but no one,
not anyone, can say what the voices mean;
they may as well mean a high-summer
blessing of awakening, a plain joy
you may also choose, and live within,
for as many days as there will be.

SIREN SONG

The older hikers are staring into the water —
it looks too hard to get down to it over the rocks —

and the woman tells her husband, it's all right,
she's close enough, she's seen enough,

but she doesn't sound convinced and he knows it, turning away;
he's tired now, but she would like to go further, as I

am going, because I still have strong legs and good boots
she envies, I suppose, almost lured to try, and then

they are gone. It takes me only a minute to clamber down
and ford the swampy inlet, wet to the waist,

and I'm swimming to the raised tip of the dead limb
at the center of Shirley Lake like one preserved past age

in the delicious chill that calls to mind
how geniuses are having their brains frozen now

against a future they trust will remember them
and sigh for their return, but what if

your brain isn't your best feature
or your noblest part, as if even the noblest skull-mass

isn't past useful freeze-drying at the point of death,
shocked too often by blips of logic or passion,

too many of its little brilliancies lost in corridors
like books misfiled in the library and therefore lost,

simply not there? So I wish my legs to be iced up instead
for striding and climbing through as much of time as I am able,

walking ahead of others as I have always left my companions
irritably lagging a yard or so behind

but haven't the bones shifted place themselves
under the sedimentary loosening sway of the spine

and the muscles come unmoored enough under the pubic bone
to make my youth unreturnable to me even in the age

when the cryogenic dead shall be raised incorruptible?
And this is why a pain shot down the leg this morning

as soon as the hiking boot went on, the sorry limb
knew it was being summoned for another test of greatness

and thought about failing graciously with a small thank-you,
staying to recline in the hotel lobby in the valley

stroked by the coffinlike plush of the sofas,
guessing at how it will be to stir inside the box for centuries

whenever the earth contracts and settles
under the compacting entrance of more and more death,

its weakest joint, the sprained V
of its gone sexual exuberance, numbing slightly

at the arrivals of beings it cannot shift or turn to nestle against
because there is always more numbing,

more separation into ever finer dust,
a decomposition as patient as this granite's into the meadow

as I swim back seriously shivering now
to sun myself, naked as a siren on the rock,

one of the immortal beauties, a warning, a temptation,
combing my silvering hair.

BURIED TREASURE

"We're always open" — Flabby arms and faces
smoking, overweight parents like Disney gnomes
comforting the baby with starchy food. The baby
is twisting around in her high chair crying
with white paste on her face. "My name is Coral" —
The non-dairy creamer stays out on the table
all day and all night, like a reef
breathing in the dark under a mile of water,
living color, the wonderful world
of color. "Can I take your order?" —
Because maybe he feels like crying too,
a little boy is twisting around from his table
to look at the baby. I remember you.
"Breakfast, breakfast 24 hours a day" — I mean,
I remember being you, at a formica table with Mom
and Grandma and big sister like you to learn
the baby had died while being born. "We never
sleep" — Sit still and quit it, says Mom,
your food will be here in a minute. But it
isn't and he's bored, reading from the menu so I
can hear. Two sausage links, two strips of bacon,
two buttermilk pancakes, two farm-fresh eggs
any style, $3.49. Reassuring food, bad for me
as childhood. "Here's your breakfast" — God,
look at her hair. Shut up, says Mom, you're about
driving me up the wall. Teased up all over
too big and wrong for the thin pouty face,

which she knows, staring up the wall away from
the painful family. Can she hear herself
talk? She hears herself whisper movie lines of
love, wind lifting her sudden blonde hair in twilight.
Mom, let me do your hair. The boy is eating
very quietly. The baby is asleep. I mean,
the baby is dead. "Is everything all right?" —
I escaped the farmbelt working class,
then a dining-room of hostile relatives
starts enacting the life I have lived all this
time, like bloated coral under the terrible sea.
"Can I get you anything else?" —   The little boy
has noticed the turquoise stud in my left ear,
a buried treasure. "We are always open" —
Quit staring at the gentleman like that.
I think I have escaped, but I want a son like you.

THE LAST HOUR OF THE NIGHT

A boy wakes up before dawn
and pulls on his clothes from the chair,
gets up and walks downstairs and sits
by the window looking into
the dark. The little furnace
rattles and ticks above the rush of flame
like matter and spirit. Light drops of rain
touch the glass. Outside in empty space,
reflected from the wall, Jesus
the protector and accuser
discloses his pierced heart.
There is a lighter darkness in the east,
a cluster of street lamps on the dark hill
in the west. The houses are rose-white,
each one a silhouette emerging into the day
alone. *I will go to the altar of God,*
to God who gives joy
to my youth. Then his mother is in the room,
he opens the door to the cold
and his clothes comfort his quivering skin,
he mouths the responses as they walk to church
without talking. *Introibo ad altare dei,*
ad deum qui laetificat
juventutem meam. He is afraid of making a mistake again,
sounding the chime at the wrong moment,
spilling the water as the priest
washes his hands for the holy rite
and chants the blessing down at him

with a look of blame. His mother
will console him with a prayer, lighting a candle
at the Blessed Mother's altar.
But he leaves her at the side entrance
and the heavy door opens, and to the solitary man
looking up from his breviary in the darkly lit room
he whispers a *good morning Father*
that can't be heard. He counts out
the wafers of bread for the tabernacle,
prepares the water and wine,
puts on the alb and surplice and the pinching
collar. The wood and stone of the sacristy
are suffused with incense, the hoarded piety
of many cold mornings. It is the hour
before day has begun and wrongs are committed,
the hour of forgiveness. This darkness
must be the presence of God.

SONG FOR TWO VOICES

An ancient and spacious desolation
unreachable by love, a wordless prayer
I remember. *Around my heart there's a pain.*
The soul wanders from the body in the night and returns
in the day: I wake up shouting at my dead friend,
I can't hear you. *Life I could not live.*
The candle a figure of the soul, his presence
fading as his deathtime grows longer. Still,
we go on talking. *Feeding and exercising and resting
my unreliable body.* Dancing, unclenching the body
and stilling the mind, abandoning perfection
to be human, everything filling with breath.
Held in my man's arms, but lonely.
A cradle, a last bed, a loss of feeling in the fingertips,
the cup of a flower stripped of petals,
the husk of the body. *To have been of help,
I should have been able to remember everything,
to bring some wisdom in.* Ashes of the dead
flung back in our faces, a foghorn mourning lostness,
a wreath of memories untied and handed to the water.
*Useless to continue, but I need to finish
what's begun.* The truth is, we have no idea
what makes any of us live. *The margin
on which we thrive, ever so slightly ahead
of the wash of decay.* The agave
blooming once after decades of life
twenty feet high in his yard as he died,
then dying itself. The olive tree,
each leaf shining separate, dark red

in late sun. *Now the garden is tended by others.*
You open the gates of dawn with wisdom,
you change the times with understanding,
you set the succession of seasons,
you arrange the stars to your will. *A web of thought and touch
and intention. The spirit who breathes life,
though daily I fail.* I was the boy who survived
by peering alone into books of maps
for a vision of escape. *I was carrying a pile of photographs
taken by a man who was leaving me,
never to be my lover.* Resting places in the tinted desert,
shelter and comfort in the names of rivers.
Where is my home? *They were mounted
behind unframed sheets of glass, I let them slip,
the edges slit my wrist.* The world etched
into jigsaw shapes, green and violet, yellow and red,
languages and minds. *Blood everywhere. Of course,
I saved the photographs. But now it's dark.*
Black birds are skimming the waves
like the edges of a loosely cast net. I pray,
return my soul to me. *Those troublesome prayers
for martyrs, the ones who go to their deaths
unfulfilled. How am I different?*
The song of a man coming apart
who lies in a half-dream pondering his way
on a map through the streets of pain.
*I like the dawn creeping through the fog, and the flat
immensity of dark nights.* Love,
the creator, whose word separates the day
from the night. *The white scars on my wrist.*

THE DEAD

Curled warm at my back asleep you wake me
crying softly in my ear
in the dark. Low clouds whirling
over the mountain. Hard rain all night
swallowed up in red earth.
Harvest time, fields burnt clean,
trucks up and down the rutted road
with loads of gnarled cane
stacked high. Sweet odor
of manured sugar plowed under.
We are alone
in the middle of the ocean
visited far from home by the dead
we have buried. So many:
they have come over the water
to remind us
in our sleep. Breath of ghosts
in the four-petalled flowers. Ghosts
in the cane. A plume of sweet smoke
from the mill stack.
Names on scraps of paper
burning. Smoke of words in dreams.
Married, bound to each other,
we have greened and prospered, two men
sorrowful over joy.

When I whisper your name you scream
that people are dying. We must be dying too.
I whisper to wake you
and you scream for light.
Hard rain all night
swallowed up in red earth.

TRUE STORY
for Bo

Darling you should contract a terminal illness he'd say
you're writing too slowly and give that Tallulah smirk,

waving a bony arm at me and flicking ash: four books
in three years, each one a lifetime past the one before,

while the virus stole his body from his mind. I could only
watch him burn, the way he'd sit and roll a clean

page into the machine and type *Chapter 1 Page 1* and pull
the most demented stories out his head from start to finish

in the proper order, each one a lifetime truer than the one
before. Now he comes to me from death in the middle of

the night as a live coal in my heart, a pang that wakes me up:
he says *Darling you want pain?* I want to turn a light on

to get hold of myself but close my eyes to stay in the dark.
He says *All right. I'll give you pain.* He says *Someday*

it just might kill you. If it's any comfort. Someday soon.

TRANSFIGURED

I was pushing my baby in the stroller up Market St.
when I passed the open door of the room you and I
made love in one slow afternoon so long ago it appeared to me
as a photograph of a doorway in a building
that's been torn down for years and replaced
with another structure. A maid's cart was waiting on the sidewalk
with brooms and disinfectants like the angel
that removes from empty rooms the history
of the human beings who have lived in them,
their gestures and cries. The baby was exuberant
as he is these days almost all his waking hours,
gripping the handlebar face up to the sun and rocking
forward and back to make the world go faster,
squealing with the anticipation of a roller coaster dip
in the terrain of his existence about to stir him more alive
at every moment. The unadorned walls
and the bedspread printed with cowboy hats and pistols and ropes
made it look like the lonely room I shared with my brother
but transfigured for a moment by our boyish light and sweat,
our comical rendezvous to be alone there
where no one would know us, your breath in my ear
asking, Will you be my brother? It is hours in the future
where you are now in a country an ocean away
but I could see the little infinite spiral of the rumpled sheets
and the bedside lamp still lit against the motionless
dark, just as we left it when we had to step back

into the afternoon of an ordinary day and walk each other
to the corner to say goodbye, too ignorant of forever
to spend tears on it. Happiness comes eventually to me
but only on condition that sadness come first,
and since I had been quiet too long
and distracted from our babbling song of the constantly moving city
the baby turned around in the stroller with an inquisitive smile
to look at me.

ASPENS

The individual life is not the point — *admire me
I am a violet*, and so on, as John Keats mocked,
in the voice of the self who wants to be more precious
than existence — long parentless by then,
nursing his brother Tom through the long bloodcoughing
months of death and knowing his own could come soon,
perhaps before love, or another visitation of poetry,
though he had only reached the Chamber of Maiden-thought
in the house of many rooms he was sketching out
in his own faint light — *on all sides many doors set open but all
dark all leading to dark passages* — maybe few to be revealed
in an individual life. So the naturalist led us poets
up a creekbed to show us a tiny portion of our own world:
a fragile meetingpoint of volcanic rock & granite
that over a hundred thousand years urged forth a way
for water to wash down and make this canyon to the valley:
told us that the grove of quaking aspens we stopped beside
ought to call into question our definition of a tree:
not separate trees but clones sprung from an underground
rhizomal oh I don't know what the word was,
which makes me ashamed — I didn't write it down — as if
knowledge of the names of things means understanding anything
of what they are — the other poets, I figured, were writing down
notes for me — wanting really to have the labeled placards
in an arboretum (*dote upon me I am a primrose*) so I could

walk away satisfied knowing more than enough but actually
nothing much. The point was that the system of roots beneath us
was vaster than we could think, a million years old or so,
and apparently so capable of continuing sending up clones each season
that it can wait for the arrival of the next ice age to this valley
if it takes another million years, and the theorizers who know
that our minds and words stop short of what this might mean
have posited what they can only call "theoretical immortality."
(All of the poets wrote *that* one down.) All right, so I returned
to poetry so late, guilty, ashamed, regretful, sad, all right.
My teacher beside me — disoriented by all these
lateblooming Sierra wildflowers unknown in northern New Hampshire —
another system but not another earth — connected underneath —
(same late-July mosquitoes here as there biting me though,
taking me back to my summers by Mt. Chocorua at the commie camp,
swimming in the deep pond there, deciding to be a writer and so
to change the world, *rich in the simple worship of a day*) — she said
she was grateful there was such a community of writers as this one
and she had found it — so little of the usual mutual hatred
and self-mistrust because we're working every day and facing
the blankness of paper, urging each other on, not showing off our
bundles of poems from home to be doted upon or angling
for career moves, though I do want my fucking book to get out
of my house. She agreed with me, no, you are not, at the age
of 45, the next young thing the poetry biz is waiting
to discover, and you can thank God herself for it, having had

students at the age of 23 all but drown in acclaim and felt
afraid for them as in, O honey — just wait until you're in
a small town somewhere with an underpaying job and a couple of
babies, not enough time, a husband who helps out, or not,
and one book on the shelf while the world has moved on
to the next bright morning star — that's when, if you're lucky,
you'll be a writer. Send down your taproot then, into the
many-chambered whatever it is, the comfort and fright of it,
that we're all connected. *And thus by every germ of Spirit*
sucking the Sap from mould ethereal every human might become great,
and Humanity instead of being a wide heath of Furse and Briars
with here and there a remote Oak or Pine, would become
a grand democracy of Forest Trees. These plant "communities" —
manzanita, huckleberry, snow-something, oh I didn't write those down
either I was so tired, the words are not the point — they're migrating
over geological time — they send messages to each other
across the great spongeous rootmass about changes in temp. and
rainfall, outbreaks of blight, accumulated experience we'd call
gossip or history, the sports and weather, film at 11 — they slowly
move, and so others move with them, what's the choice — the point
is the interwoven indistinguishableness that all life feeds
and is fed by, not the individual life. And the hope
that I will be communicated with among the forms of life
must be what is meant by a blessing — say, the man I saw
laying his hands on another man's head, in the rain, to bless him,
in a crowd at the corner of Post & Stockton in the middle of the day —

it must be only our bodies, our skin, that make us think
we are contained in one place in one self, as a tree appears to end
at the root, the rock, the leaf-edge, the air, as a mountain appears
to end at the level ground, so we need the laying on
of hands to make an entryway into the one
oh what will I call it? We don't even have the same desires
as ourselves, as when the ex-President said, "I have opinions
of my own. Strong opinions. But I don't always agree with them."
We are temporary shadows constantly turning around
to misremember, elaborate constructions
unrecoverable a moment later, contradictory lifelines
in the palms of our hands. So even a sad song causes happiness
when it comes from the heart. So Jacob asked a blessing of his father
as I did, though I too had to steal it, holding his hand as he died
in a coma in a narrow bed: still, I think he was waiting for me.
And afterwards we go on living, at our own mercy,
which can be short at hand. Am I too old?
I am not the next young thing but that has never stopped
the subterranean-stream-continuation of all the desires.
Band of rose gold on my finger, and 16 years of marriage
to the man I love, faithful in our quotes open relationship
well are we? though openness can be an aperture or chasm. The man
handing me change in the hardware store with my wall-grabbers
and wingnuts had two nipple rings, which I thought was one
too many, and was young enough to be my child; he made me hot
as our hands met though it meant nothing much, and am I too old

to get a nipple ring? I want to ask him if I did that would it
hurt, but a part of me I love is afraid it might not hurt enough:
more unfulfillment in desire, even the desire for pain, which runs on
in the underground stream and resurfaces each season
in its fashion, as here in a brightly-lit store midday
on Castro St.: I wanted to lick the salt from his skin.
Oh what would I turn into if I were single again? The devious
frightened loner I was before. Undiscovered by poetry.
Now we look upward on the trail because the life of birds,
living or ornamental, this one or the birds of tapestry in the decor
of our minds, the nothing that is not there, and the nothing
that is — their life is song. A junco but I didn't see it,
the guide helped us notice and then I heard it, a scold, a
trailing-off *compleynt*, as Bela Bartók must have heard
the actual Hungarian birds of his youth that he lived among
before the disaster of our midcentury dispersed the forms of life
but how did he still hear them and place them
directly by their song and without names into that never-quite-
finished Piano Concerto No. 3, his cry of anguished love
and a capitulation before some wellspring he knew would continue
after him, or at any rate that's what I heard when I first
heard it in Ann Arbor some twenty years ago, the days when I
was almost giving up on my own soul and living in that piss-
smelling boarding house on Miller Avenue, mourning my first lover,
smoking so much dope, back in the closet again,
romanticizing Larry and Sadie the drunks from the U. P. next door

because they were Indians and had done so much Real Time
in the Washtenaw County Jail right across the street —
we heard the screams and fighting of the prisoners at night —
and who therefore seemed to live more intensely, have *more* life,
than one such as me writing termpapers on *Middlemarch*,
when what I wanted from them really was another sedative drug —
what a sorrowful young youth I was, pitiful jade plant in my window
likewise half in love with death, but I had a rainsoaked *Book of*
Nightmares and the birds that Bela Bartók conjured up for me,
one mortal body passing the song on to another
across indefinite time, his final music, so full of legend and glory,
sitting on a cot an almost penniless refugee in 1945 on W. 57th St.
in New York knowing he was dying, racing to leave it
as a birthday present for his wife and even more, a useful
concert-piece that she could go on playing and earn a little
money from to make her way, the sheet music found only later
lying out of order on every available surface of bed and desk
and floor, a windowless room in which he caused
the birds of gone-forever Hungary to go on singing.

NOT THERE
(1963)

The boy can't find it
on the hand-me-down   battered globe

tracing his fingers across the blue nothing

and over the tiny green backs
of mountains   come out of the sea

Okinawa   Formosa
    French Indochina   Siam

black letters raised up as though names
    were actual scars

and would a father forsake his child?

On the TV set
a man in a bright robe is burning
just sitting in the road there
burning

like someone gone God-crazy
falling out in church
like someone blocking his path to say

This life is sanctified
This life is nothing

The war is in Vietnam
but Vietnam isn't there

So he can only guess his father has left the earth.

PASSAGE

> *(Daniel Kehoe, my great-great-grandfather,*
> *St. Louis, 1876)*

Wagonloads of barrels at the warehouse docks —
black river water passing —
men calling across the levee from barges into the dark,
wet as the pavingstones
worn smooth by the mud and gravel of wheels in the rain,
empty shopstalls under the gas light, the last of it
before the coming awake of the Soulard Market
where he sat with her that first time of a Sunday, shyly,
and walked her home to Laclede Street carrying her parcel
of onions and flowers, and her ma'am at the door with a sharp look
for she'd have no visits from men, and such a low one,
in his workworn coat and his wagoner's cap —
All but Sunday he labors into the dawn
hauling barrels from the brewer's to the river —
the horses stir at the trough as they drink, and stamp,
and let out such steaming breaths as there's a fire in them
as he takes down the last of the load, looking downriver
at the New Orleans boat they both found passage on
their separate times, on a promise of what work
their kind could be allowed —
Just now in the last of the dark she must be rising
to tend the kitchen fire and ready the meal
before her people's children wake,
but may it be she will come to care for him,
for without a man she will never leave that house,

and such a life
she can't have left her mother for in the county of Cork —
She will be lighting a candle over the room to St. Bridget
when she wakes, to protect her soul,
to keep her loved ones safe,
because her people never let her out for church but Sunday
and she must feel the peril of it, the darkness of that house —
O my dear dead father in Ireland he prays,
the light coming as a mist on the farther shore,
and time to be starting back:
May it happen she will think of me.

SAINTS BEHIND GLASS

(San Cristóbal de las Casas, Chiapas, Mexico)

I.

Santa María with a halo of silver rays
and twelve swords in her heart,

Santo Muerte, broken-bone Christ weeping
painted tears of blood:

ancestors, first weavers, saints
who walked the earth at the beginning of time
and speak in dreams:

In a darkened chapel at the center of the world
they watch now and listen, standing very still —

water-mother with a skirt of jade,
sky-father with a crown of stars —

the conquered moon and sun.

◆

Behind the church
a man selling earthen jars and *animalitos*
in the tin-roofed patio of his house
offers me a taste of *posh* —

above him on the family altar

Our Lady of Sorrows
in a red *huipil* and black skirt
woven by hand —

A strong liquor of sugarcane.
He tells me *The drink*
knows what the saints know —
It gives me knowledge —

Church bells mark the hour,
one bell at the end out of tune
like a demon's joke —

I answer *no thank you* and he says *O — un religioso —*
some kind of holy man.

◆

Up the Avenida Insurgentes
comes a procession
to the cathedral,
thirty men, women and children in dark shawls
following a hearse
with a small child's casket,

the afternoon downpour
turning streets to streams now
and spilling from the mouths of lions

in the eaves —
hailstones clatter like flung toys —

then a sky-clearing over the mountains —
the ochre stone glistens as they enter it.

◆

Today the ruling party
of Institutional Revolution
has set up a tent in the park,
a free medical *consultorio*, a haircut and shave stand,
a table of free food, bags of corn meal and rice.
The man inside is almost pleading through the megaphone,
calling onlookers to come over, not to hold back:
we are here to show you the *beneficios*
the *partido* can extend
to the *población*. But only the food
draws a few passers-by. And they go quickly away.

II.

What have you dreamed? the shaman asks
in the church of Chamula
where Mass is no longer said.
Does someone want to harm you?
Have you worshipped well?
She takes the infant's pulse,
holds out a mirror

to capture the evil,
sounds a tiny whistle
to call back the soul
from its fright —

We are in the sacred mountain,
pine needles and palms and flower petals
strewn over the floor —
across the vault of heaven
stars are painted on the wooden beams,
a bull and jaguar and lion, an eagle and snake —
arranged along the walls behind glass
the saints observe the soul-healing,
little mirrors strung from their necks —

Under the baptismal font
that is covered and hidden away beside the door
the older children play cat's cradle with white string.
Mal de ojo. A child can so easily lose its soul.
The parents have brought candles and eggs,
three bottles of Pepsi
and a bottle of *posh*,
a chicken in return for the child's
animal spirit. The shaman
rubs an egg over the crying body
to cleanse it of harm. Drinking,
calling, chanting a prayer, calling out,
entering a trance —

◆

We are watching the TV with no sound at a family food stall, eating *taquitos* with orange Fanta, everyone in the commercials very beautiful and white. In the '50s, says Mercedes, whose mother can cure the evil eye, the party chose a few men from Chamula and taught them Spanish, how to read and write, made them into local bosses who control the land and the stores now, the sale of *posh*, the vote on election day. They've spread the word that Pepsi is more powerful than water and the Protestants favor sodas over *posh*, of course, though people just mix the two. *Evangelistas*, she sniffs. As many as stones on the road. Always calling you *dear brother*. Over the radio Nat King Cole is singing "Cielito Lindo" and I think of Ritchie Valens, a Mexican kid from L.A. who wanted to record "La Bamba," asking his manager *If Nat King Cole can sing in Spanish why can't I?* Once, says Mercedes, I took a blonde-haired Mexican to Chamula because she wanted to see a shaman. She offered 30,000 pesos but the shaman refused, even after the woman offered to pay less, to show she was sincere. We hop onto a *colectivo*; two women in dark shawls are on their way to the home of the child who has died.

III.

Fray Bartolomé de las Casas
watches over the Indians of the market,

barefoot girls
who have come down the mountain
with bundles of firewood
on their backs —

a man of prayer and knowledge
a rich man
who renounced his *encomienda*
on the island of Cuba — *encomendar*,
to entrust, a way of saying
to enslave —
who refused slave owners the sacraments,
who argued, against Aristotle,
that Indians are not slaves by nature,
whose books were burned as heresy by the viceroy
in the *zócalo* of Mexico City,
who proved powerless against the landowners
and his Church,
who returned to Spain
a man of seventy
to go on fighting,
four hundred years now —

the good brother mourns
among the plane trees in the quiet square
in his bronze shroud.

◆

By the bus station
a man with guitar is singing
Mi casa se derrumbió
porque faltaban tus brazos.
A man from the rainforest to the east,
a Lacandon, listens,
perhaps not understanding
the words.
His hair is long and dark and uncombed.
He wears a white tunic,
no pants, old boots.
The men at the desk
selling tickets to Palenque
make fun of him, asking
¿Cómo te llamas? with stern faces
as if addressing a child,
and shyly, half-smiling,
he draws away.
You don't have a name? one says.
I'm not telling you, he says.

◆

The presidential candidate's speech
in a headline of the *Excelsior*:
MAS BIENESTAR Y RESCATE
DE LA CONFIANZA POPULAR;
ES INAPLAZABLE LA RENOVACION:

It's the latest word, says Mercedes,
la renovación — new this, new that —
remodeling, redecoration,
reupholstery —
I am buying a woven bag from Tenejapa for my *tallit*,
a bread cloth for Shabbat
from San Andrés Larráinzar
bordered with the red and gold pattern
of the corn god,
the four-cornered sky crossed by the sun,
the *sukkat shalom*,
the shelter of peace.

IV.

Incense, the resonant hum
after the sounding of bells,
a pale white Jesus and Mary
in pink native dress
inside a shrine of glass,
San Lorenzo adorned with mirrors
and holy ribbons
to guard his soul —

Gloria dejo en memoria
y estas razones aquí
de que no llore por mí

de que no llore por mí
porque me quita la gloria —

Gloria le digo a Dios
y que conmigo sea bueno
porque también en el cielo
porque también en el cielo
nos hemos de ver los dos

y en este trance veloz
ya yo cumplí mi destino
y en la gloria entraré
en la gloria entraré
purificado y divino —

By a side-altar covered with flowers,
a circle of candles
burning in glass on the floor,
women kneel on the stone
of the cathedral
to pray —

Hush dear mother —
don't weep now — goodbye —
I have gone to the saints of God —
don't weep now —
don't steal my glory —
God will guard you — don't cry —

*Pure as God I go back to glory,
pure as God I leave glory behind —
God be good now to me,
because I will have to see
because I will have to see you
in the sky —*

And beside them, three men are playing —
at times the sound is lost
to *marimbas* and fireworks in the square —
playing a violin, a guitar, a handmade harp
boxlike as a little coffin —

they were chosen by the saints,
they were taught in dreams
to weep this music —

a friars' hymn
of the sixteenth century,
a haunted lament
of rising and falling tones,
terribly slow,
a prayer of resolute sadness
and humbled heart,
a *despedimiento del angelito*,
a vigil for the child
who will not return.

BRAND NEW

for Charlie Halloran

1.

One of these mornings you're going to rise up singing —
Now Charlie's body is surrounded by
the work of his hands,
his hats and painted scarves
arrayed around him on the bed,
and on a tape from long ago he plays the flute
as we gather in the house — "Summertime"
in February light —   All night he moaned
and vomited, sloughing off the body one agony
after another and his mind already at play somewhere,
talking to people we couldn't see in words
we couldn't hear until he stirred
a last time to come back — "hold me," he said,
and carefully David held his hands — he didn't much like
being touched any more — it hurt — "no, hold me,"
he said — so David lay beside him on the sheet
to cradle the sore bones and as one died
the other slept, worn out from the long night,
the work of love come to an end
and so much work undone.

2.

In the middle of Joah's dance bowling balls
start careening across the stage, two or three
at first and it's more or less manageable to nudge them
off, even make a pleasing pattern of the interruption
and go on dancing, then it's happening much
faster than he can catch and guide them and at last
he has to give in and choose just one, set his fingers
inside and caress it, toss it into the air
and at its highest point the camera catches it
to make the photo next to Charlie's bed, Joah
gazing up in delight and unburdened after all
though he's long dead — the bowling ball
fell into his arms, and he lugged the weight away.

3.

How do we forgive ourselves for what
we haven't done? The failures of courage
and heart, so much undared and un-
expressed —   Over and over we talked about it,
the ways we hadn't measured up, done what
we'd told ourselves by now we would.
Charlie showed me once a little potted orchid
on his table, four pale blooms

like crumpled paper cups turned over — "the story
of my life," he said, trying to smile,
furious that day at what he'd given up on and have to
give up next, what would be taken away. First
the strength of his hands to sew and paint
and play music. Then his sight. Then his breath.
Then he *did* smile. "Fucking thing
only came this far and didn't open."
Taped to the wall there is Adrienne's letter
urging, believing, "Yes,
you must continue," and what if our lives
are forgotten, and what if we're lost? We live on
in others but they will also die, and one day
it will be as if none of us had lived. I want to believe,
when everything that was given to us is taken
back, love remains, and won't forget.

4.

Living without knowing, and every day
starting all over again —   One day I saw him
on 18th Street, bundled in scarves
under the bright sun as if noon were
midnight and leaning at his cane and I moved
to kiss him until he snapped, "You can't do that,"
his voice gone harsh because
he'd had to say this now

too many times. Of course. I remember.
I can't kiss you any more. It was Pesach —
in the doctor's office he'd just approached the moment of death
in a waking dream, a spirit leading him to a wall
and to a door in the wall he had to open —
and there was a great cry in the land of Egypt,
for there was not a house where there was not one dead.
We had to begin again,
light the candles of the seder another year
and remember for each other the promise of freedom,
joining hands. Then Charlie read in the Haggadah
the voice of a child asking, "What good
will these rituals ever do for me?," and rushed away.
The orchids he had brought for the table
were a ritual, too, and as he cried
in the next room in his sister's arms
we looked at them,
ashamed of prayers made of words.

5.

Hey babe: I greet you sitting in the sun
in your window seat, catching morning light,
threading tiny green beads on a string
to decorate your velvet hat: in the middle of the city
you're a bird of magic in the flowering branches
of a forest, impatient spirit, girl-boy, gay one,

beautiful and frail, with a button on your favorite cap
that says *Destination Unknown* — you're going out tonight
in rouge and a velvet dress and beaded hat
and the room's in a riot, sewing machines and hat blocks,
ironing boards and metal presses, wigs,
spray paint in cans, church hats for your nurses
from the hospital, spools of thread on pegs,
pattern books and fashion magazines, buttons and
sequins, feathers and painted silk, shells and ribbons,
polished stones — You are home. You are transformed.
You tell me an angel spoke to you
when you were a child, telling you God is love,
the love of your family you will always have with you:
hold fast to it and trust it and believe it.
Both our fathers think we've thrown away our faith now
and how can we explain we haven't turned away
but returned by different paths, fairy, pantheist, Jew,
because even though we're full of doubt
doubt dissatisfies us — *We praise the source of life*
who has kept us alive, and sustained us,
and brought us to this time. We're so old we're brand new.

No olvides, boricua,
cuando el viento raspa
los proyectos
con lenguas de alambre
que tu patria es una india cautiva
¿y tu?
Semilla dormida....

    Ricardo Alonso, "Abuela y patria"

... an island blest by obscurity, cherishing our
insignificance....

    Derek Walcott, *The Antilles*

DELLE AVENUE

1.

It looks unfamiliar, it looks the same, my lost country,

kids in plaid uniforms just getting out of Mission Grammar for the afternoon
    but no one on my street,

no one home, no answer at 51 where Tony lives,

dying now — same yellowed curtains drooping, that storm window still hanging
    loose

in the same place, unfixed, a bad fit: It's a ghost town: In a dream I'd moved
    back in

and opened the Coldspot to find the little frosted-up freezer still had no door,
    a wide-open

frozen heart: The Iglesia de Dios is repainted now from the fire

but the steeple's gone: Someone condo'd the little mansion at the corner but
    it's sagging into history again,

still for sale, paint peeling off and windows broken: The neighborhood was
    going to come back,

the new train line's in where they leveled Roxbury Crossing for the expressway
    that never got built,

a three-mile swath of houses and a shopping district, twenty years a barren
    corridor:

Now the empty frightening corner of Columbus and Tremont's a regular vision
    of grace,

green landscaping and a chrome-and-glass station under crime lights

where the homeless cadge cigarettes and sleep, and they call the place Roxbury
    Crossing again

as if the dead will sit up and speak, the past unlost: It's strange to me but this
    is how I remember it,

icicles starting on the stiff little trees after cold rain, brave stalwart
    clapboards

and a plain brick row for the Irish poor of 1871 looking to come up in the
    world, a big tenement on the corner

with no front door, no heat, no water, old shirts and towels stuffed into the
    window cracks

and people in and out of it all night, three lots cleared by arson, one

rehab'd by the block committee as a playground for the toddlers and junkies, a
    pretty place,

a nice bad part of town marooned between armed towers of public housing:
    The young professionals moved

a mile down the line to Jamaica Plain instead, they've passed this poor street
    by, an avenue,

one-way and three blocks long: If you miss the last turn you dead-end into a
    weed lot of charred wood

and roof scraps, the "meadow," a cracked stairway rising to the old convent on
    the next

street up the hill and the ledge where kids drink and break glass and look at
    the view, the glittering skyline

where the money must have gone, Harvard's medical center where three-decker
    houses used to sit

and the medical power plant erected on top of protests and cries, a plume of
    diesel smoke

like a string of unsuccessful lawsuits, the Elegance #2 Unisex and La Preferida
    Superette, the Giant Valu

closed down by the Health Department, the record shop and botánica, the
    drugstore boarded up

ever since a holdup crew shot the owner dead, the Irish funeral home,

the Mission Hill project clustered behind the spires of the Mission Church like
    a candlelight

procession, like the altar of crutches left with Our Lady of Perpetual Help,
    warring boom-boxes

jamming up the street playing sólo tu que-RER, yo quisiera SER, so
    DON'T-push-me-cause-I'm-close-

to-the-EDGE: I'm-TRY-in'-not-to-LOSE-my-head, mi vida yo no tengo la
    culpa, and a police car

tears up Tremont spinning a blue alarm: It's years ago: It's that time of the
    evening when there's still

light in the sky but close in it's getting dark in the shadows of Delle Avenue,
    and it's time to go home.

2.

— *the wind began to switch* — / the lights
go down / on a crowd of eight ten twelve
year old children / going nuts / and in

a Puerto Rican village / Dorotea and her aunt
talk over the future / island music playing
in the square / feathered dancers raking

earth with bare feet / seeds in the memory
to be carried into exile / north to ice-hard
streets / oh *tía* / do we have to leave

our home / — *the house began to pitch* — /
a wind that pulls up palm trees / a strong
wind / you can't fight it / it's a better

life up there / people shouting *¡corran!* /
¡corran! / ya viene el huracán / a wind
that can lift you up *negrita* / and carry you

away / you are inside it / the great storm
of underdevelopment / children of runaway slaves
wheeled around in its eye with the trees

and the roots / the central poles of home /
it's war / and the rumors of war / and it's
rocking the house / an auditorium packed with

tough and awestruck children / oh *tía* where
are you / I'm cold in the northeast wind / it's
me on this empty stage / it happened to me: — /

then here's a man / got tin music coming out a
box / gonna rock the house / good fairy in a
dress / working rouge onto big boned cheeks /

Cuban scarecrow / sleeping on newspaper on a
stoop in the project / dreaming of *un cerebro
pa' pensar* / gangster lion in a sharp hat

polishing his car / waiting for his number to
hit / *en la lotería* / don't cry *niña* / we'll take
care of you / *ya no estás en tu islita* / you never

seen a play before? / no you in Mission Hill now
girl / *son los Junided Stays* here / and it's opening
night / Diana backstage managing the hurricane

dance / the musical cues / the third-graders in
munchkin clothes / Elena down in the audience
holding the roof on / excitement at the edge of

riot / we're sweating like mad / *carajo* / we
better put on a *show* / wicked Maxine with a
crazy laugh / from raising three kids alone on

AFDC / belts out Don't You Bring Me No Bad News
in a voice that stills the house / Dorotea sings
a quiet lament / and in the front rows I see

tears / but they know how the story goes / how
her new friends in the city all lost
something too / and *el mago de Oz* is just

an idiot precinct boss / dispensing promises /
and evil melts away / in a bucket of water
and the little girl goes home / *pero* she's still

got to move with her *tía* to Boston only she knows
it's going to work out now *¿verdad?* / freedom you
see / has got our hearts singing so joyfully / just

look about / you owe it to yourself to check it out /
can't you feel a / brand new day / and the curtain
falls to hollers and cheers / me and Tony help

the kids wipe off the makeup / walk them
up front to meet their parents and fans / we
did it / the whole neighborhood turned out / we

did it / for once / and later / on the street
it's another hot night / men stretched out on
car hoods smoking reefer / under a street lamp /

white kids in front of the pizza shop / trying
to look black / Dominicans roasting a
side of pork in a back lot / playing *merengue*

loud / Alice at her third-floor window with
two of her cats / muttering over the class of
people coming in / only thank the Blessed Mother

my Harry didn't live to see / and here is my
front door again / my two rooms / my quiet
shelter / — *the house began to twitch* — / fire-

crackers or a backfire or gunshots / garbage
falling from upper windows / water running /
metal punk from next door through the brick

wall / — *the room began to pitch* — / and that smell
on the air / as though it's just rained hard / or is
about to / a strong wind stirring / and sweet

3.

A crossing, a crossroads, a boundary, a border line:

A horse-and-wagon stop, a railroad station, a streetcar switch, a court-ordered bus route, a meeting of the ways,

A light snow is falling,

It falls on the abandoned breweries, it falls on the empty lots where the tannery and the grist mill stood, the sunken footings of the car-horse stables and the railroad shops, it buries the tracks,

It graces the windward side of the Bromley Heath project, and from his farm William Heath organizes the Roxbury Minutemen who will fight in the Battle of Lexington, and the snow covers the windowless cars abandoned at the foot of the hill:

A fair and handsome country towne, well wooded and watered, having a clear and fresh brook running through it; — up westward from the towne it is something rocky, whence it hathe the name of Roxberry:

And the ledge of Peter Brigham's farm is quarried away, and a row of puddingstone cottages for the tradesmen who work at the crossing goes up at the foot of the dell, a dell with an extra e tacked onto the end of it, a little flourish, or a little mistake,

Gas lights on the street like holding a match up in a dark room, and the snow swirling up at the light,

And General Washington holds a war council in Colonel Brinley's drawing room, and the Ursuline Sisters take refuge there from the fanatics of Somerville who have burned their convent to the ground, and at last the Redemptorist Fathers tear down the mansion to build their mission church on Tremont Street,

Tremont, meaning three mountains,

The hard blue clay and bedrock, the stream, the fish-weir, the summer encampment of the tribes, the gathering place, all deeded away for ten dollars to Dudley and Stoughton by Charles Josiah, called Wampatuck,

And the snow covers the sumac and the honey locusts in the sloping meadow at the top of the hill, John Parker's farm, the highest place in all the city, the harbor islands to the east and the open ocean, and new spires going up on the church to the north,

A bronze plaque is placed at the side altar for Miss Grace Hanley who lives in the Boyle house at Parker Street, cured, August 18, 1883, and her leg braces are mounted beside it,

She worked in the Back Bay, you know, when she first came over from Garwick, taking care of the little children in the big houses; my grandfather worked in a store in the South End, then they got married, he got a job with the police department and they bought a house up on Pontiac St., it was the greatest place then for the Irish, they came here because of the church,

So when I was in the South I thought the North was exciting and pretty, everyone told me but my mother didn't encourage me, no, she told me not to get into city life, I was very nervous, me and my friend was very nervous, we came from North Carolina by bus,

Y los buildings grandes que en Santo Domingo no lo habían, y todas las costumbres acá, y el frío, y el inglés,

And the snow covers the embankment that was the Stony Brook, it falls on the abolitionist's house which at last becomes the Home for Aged Colored People, then is boarded up, then burns to the ground one night in an hour,

A fire takes the factory where our grandmothers made shoes for the Yankee for three dollars a week, and the landlord pours gasoline in the basement of 44 Delle and puts a flame to it,

A child finds a needle in the snowy sand and brings it to the teacher, a child in a doorway hawks ten-dollar beads of crack —

And you know what a white lady told me?, she said, Oh, we used to drive through the project at Christmas time, to see the windows, everybody used to have their lights in the windows, and the snow falling up and down Smith Street, oh, you live in a beautiful place, and I said to myself, Honey, maybe it *was*,

Water coming down in my kitchen, just pouring down, water running down my pipes, and at night — you can hardly sleep for these cars spinning at night —,

I wish I had some pictures of it when I first moved here, it was beautiful, beautiful, we had trees and grass, and the snow continues to fall on the trees and grass,

And I don't know if you remember but this black lady lived on Ward St.?, she was threatened at night, a fire broke out in her house and she refused to move and she *didn't* move, they gave her police around the clock and that's how they broke that barrier, she was the first one in the project, and a crowd circles the building and the fire flares up at the falling snow,

But when I came I had no friends: soy de Puerto Rico y allí fue que me crié y todito, it was winter, no leaves on the trees, all alone in the apartment while the landlady went out to work y la boiler se dañó y en ese entonces iba a tener la bébé y la casa muy fría, looking out the window and wanting to go back to my country, and I would have if it hadn't been so far away,

So now the house is totally destroyed, it's not rentable, so it gets burned because it's cheaper to burn it down and corrupt the insurance, so then you have a boarded-up, burnt-up house or an empty lot and it gives you a mental picture of defeat, you can't put it into words but in your mind it's what is happening,

And do you think I would move out of here?, I would like hell leave, no sir, this is my home until the Lord takes me out of it: I could have gone to West Roxbury, I could have gone any place, no I am really going to stay here until the end of time,

And the snow falls day after day until the city comes to a stop, kids building
    fortresses and tunnels in the street and neighbors coming out of houses
    to meet each other,

A crossroads, a crossing-place, a border line covered over with snow.

4.

The same dream kept returning to me, like a lost soul at night wanting more,
    wanting more life,

or rather the dream kept coming *from* me because it was *my* soul:

that my tiny pared-down apartment, monastic cell, place of pride, was
    suddenly larger,

had been larger all along and these two rooms led to an entire room or more
    I'd failed to notice were there

or hadn't dared to enter: some dark passage, stairway, unmarked door, quick
    turn or change of vision

would lead more easily than by day I could have thought into a place of more
    light:

the dream kept changing but it was the same dream: two little rooms on a
    narrow street

led into the whole world made whole again: the compartments of one life joined

into a neighborhood of love as the night follows into morning-time: Now the light returns and a passing radio

wakes me up, it sings *No tengo casa y me mato haciendo casa de otro*, returns me to

the happiness of solitude in my little place and the undertow of wanting more but wanting more

of what? There is a map of the city of Boston on the wall beside the little clawfoot tub where I take my morning bath,

the tub facing out to the fire escape, an iron ladder leading nowhere into the air, the map disappearing

in the steam from the bath but still more real to me I think than the actual city, the names of streets

instead of streets, fine colored lines set into place some forty years ago like a picture-city,

like an enclosed room, like a dream of life instead of life, the dream of a half-bulldozed place

raised back up: streets where the houses are all pulled down now, whole neighborhoods

improved away like the gone West End that sent half my neighbors here,
>   Diana whisked away to summer camp

"at the *bright* age of 12" as if into a dream and returning home to find a crane
>   and wrecking ball where her house had stood:

now here we stand, and when they tried to take down *these* streets we held our
>   ground

and won: but still such distance between the dream of home and home: just
>   buildings:

just streets: whose dream is it: someone else owns them and we pay the rent
>   but I think

I will never leave this place, I think it must be the only home I'll have: I dress
>   and drink my coffee

from the best and oldest cup with its handle chipped off, the one that survived
>   of the set,

and walk the three blocks to the project to a scrawled-over metal door in a
>   brick wall,

a door once painted a cheery primary yellow and blue, battered like a fortress
>   now, a door without a sign,

where a roomful of children waits for me, like all the work in the world
>   remaining to be done.

5.

The world as it is, the world as I imagined it —

what do you dream, what do you imagine —

the world transformed, the world as it is,

where I turn a corner one hot summer morning
        into a little avenue —

the shapes of houses, the shapes of thoughts,
        melting together a little in the humid air —

what do you imagine, what do you wish for, what do you dream —

if not a home just a place I might afford to live —

the world I dreamed up, the world in front of my face —
        the world transformed, the world as it is —

a line separating the two like woman and man, white and black,
        grownup and child, straight and not —

the city is split, the world, split, our imaginations, split —

what do you imagine, what do you wish for, what do you expect —

working for next to nothing, not expecting much,
        expecting love in a theoretical time to come,

childlessly caring for children all day and organizing a union,
    knocking on doors with the union paper
        like a missionary with the truth —

there's the world as we want it, and there's the world we've got —

timid survivor out to change the world
    and everything changes

but the world doesn't change very much —

horny, starving, now and then a man in my bed
    who leaves in the morning, *what do you expect,*

wanting to love, not expecting much —

what do you imagine when you are working, what do you want —

just to change our childhood,
    just to dismantle the world and start over with the way
        the spirit and the mind are fed —

the real world, the world we never had —

and one summer morning I turn up a little avenue —
    woman leaning on her window sill
        to check the day's sky

says you're a nice boy, I can tell —

loud little TV blaring the *telenovela* out the corner store,
        black and white kids hollering over stickball,
            actually playing on the same block,
      guy on a stoop offering me speed under his breath —

the world as it is, melting alongside a somewhat faster world
      in his mind —

an island in the city, a little shabby, a little avenue set apart,
      a little beautiful, a little unsafe at night,

a little place for rent, two rooms, plank floors, brick walls,
      ascetic, charming, cheap,
a little bathtub facing a couple of little bullet holes
      out on the fire escape —

the world as I imagined it, the world as it is —

the neighbors are painters and dancers, Little Sisters of the Poor,
      houseful of gay boys in a punk band,
a mom who puts on plays with the kids in the street,
      a mom from Puerto Rico running for Congress —

what do you wish for, what do you imagine, what do you want —

just to remake the world, starting with our street —

and I see a shy boy peeking from behind an upstairs curtain,
      the veil of separation between worlds —

I know you, child —

what do you imagine, what do you dream —

I know the world is split, the city is split, our imaginations are split —

tell me a story,

tell me the way we close our eyes one morning and reopen them
        at the center of the world,
                the world transformed, the world as it is,

the way a person comes to know another,
        the way a person changes to someone new,

the way a story springs out of the heart all at once in many languages,
        fashioning a heaven of words among us in the air —

what do you dream, what do you imagine —

just to make the world as real as it is, and ourselves as real in it as we are.

NOTES TO THE POEMS

The quotation beginning on line 16 of "A messenger spirit" is taken from James Schuyler's poem, "Thursday," from *A Few Days* (New York: Random House, 1985).

"Aspens" is indebted to David Lukas, Tavia Cathcart, Cleopatra Mathis and Robert Hass. The italicized passages are taken from the letters of John Keats.

"Song for two voices" was inspired and shaped by, and contains quotations from, a letter from Paul Quin.

"Saints behind glass" is set in 1987, a time well before the Zapatista uprising in Chiapas but full of signs of grievance and disaster, and of change to come.

Special thanks to Elena Harap Dodd and Streetfeet Women, Diana Sabella, and Dolly DeSimone of the Parker Hill Branch, Boston Public Library, for their help in the writing of "Delle Avenue." Section III of the poem is indebted to *I Never Will Forget: Oral Histories of Mission Hill* (Boston: Action for Boston Community Development, 1980), compiled from interviews conducted by neighborhood high school students. The final line of Section V is my paraphrase of a statement by Gary Snyder in *The Real Work: Interviews and Talks 1964-1979* (New York: New Directions, 1980).